SSH... IT HAPPENS

RURAL RHYMES FROM RYME INTRINSECA

First Published in Great Britain 2016 by Mirador Publishing

Copyright © 2016 by Jan Millward

First edition: 2016

A copy of this work is available through the British Library.

ISBN: 978-1-911044-72-7

Mirador Publishing
Mirador
Wearne Lane
Langport
Somerset
TA10 9HB

Ssh..It Happens!
Rural Rhymes from Ryme Intrinseca.

By

Jan Millward

Introduction

There are folk who live in the country and there are folk who farm. Those involved in farming are a rare breed indeed. The need for humour and a sense of the ridiculous in sometimes very difficult situations is part and parcel of the job.

The equipment may have changed and the landscape from the idyllic farmyard scenes of yesteryear, but farmers are still the beating heart of the countryside.

I live in a small tied cottage with my tractor driver husband on a beef and arable farm in Dorset.

Nowadays my role involves standing in gaps, feeding the chickens and taking sandwiches to far flung fields, but the many years of agricultural college and working on farms all over the country and abroad have left me with wonderful experiences and a special understanding and appreciation of our Great British farmers.

I hope you enjoy this little book of verse. I have had great fun putting it together!

Just another day at the office!

A day in the life...

Dirty fingers,
ingrained hands.
Years of working on the land.
Calves need feeding,
milking's done,
breakfast's waiting,
the day's begun.
Steaming coffee,
Lots of toast,
bacon sandwiches
I love most.
Weather forecast,
not much rain.
Bales need moving,
out again.
Milk and calf nuts,
then some bedding,
gates need fixing,
hay wants tedding.
Grease the baler,
move the rams,
order diesel,
grade the lambs.
Scrape the slurry

into the lagoon,
wash the yard down,
whistle a tune.
Phone starts ringing,
reps again,
they'll have to wait
'till we get rain.
Scrape a knuckle,
swear a bit,
cowman says
the hay is fit.
Tanker comes
and blocks the yard,
feed rep calls
and leaves a card.
Neighbour wants
to use the truck,
the battery's flat
he's out of luck.
Grab a sandwich
a flask of tea,
there's hardly time
to have a pee.
Cows are grazing,
sun is high,
love this farming,
that's no lie!

If you have ever worked on a farm I can guarantee you will have done most, if not all of this!

Have you ever been a farmer?

Have you ever gone out lambing in pyjamas and your wellies?
Visited the bank man who didn't know that pigs were smelly?
Have you ever picked the cow muck that had dried upon your face,
or checked the sheep to find that they had vanished without trace?

Have you ever run inside the house, left boots outside the door,
not noticing your socks were full of silage bits and straw.
Have you ever slipped whilst chasing a heifer or a cow,
and cursed the living daylights as you land upon the plough.

Have you ever straddled fences connected to the mains?
Then screamed and hollered loudly, but have only you to blame.
Have you ever tried to feed a calf that doesn't want to suck,
been butted, knocked and battered when it's not your day for luck.

Have you ever faced a heifer who won't come in the shed?
Been kicked and it's not funny when they sh*t upon your head.
Have you ever skinned your knuckles trying to mend the plough,
and hopped around the farm yard saying everything but "ow".

Have you ever dropped your mobile whilst standing in warm slurry,
just when you need to ring the vet and you are in a hurry.
Have you ever got the tractor stuck a million miles from home,
had to climb the nearest hillside to get a signal on your phone.

Have you gone out for an evening and realised that your hands,
are ingrained black with oil and muck from working on the land.
there are many people out there who don't see what we do,
I'd like to get them out here and change their point of view!

Have you ever sat there listening to your friends complaining about how hard they work? Have you ever felt the urge to offer them a week on the farm, mid lambing or harvest?

Hard work

Hard work isn't sat in an office,
working nine to five each day,
with coffee breaks and lunch times
and a packet full of pay.

Hard work is when you are so tired
you don't have the strength to wash.
You lie on the bed in a stupor,
as if you've been hit by a cosh.

Hard work is three am milkings,
getting kicked in the head by a cow.
Going back out late for a calving,
still going but not knowing how.

Hard work is three weeks of lambing,
working all of the day and the night.
You don't even look in the mirror,
you know you're a scary rough sight.

Hard work is three months of harvest,
relentless days in the sun.
Working on late in the evening
until the new day has begun.

Hard work is shearing five hundred
feisty Welsh mountain sheep,
with blisters on your fingers
it's enough to make you weep.

Hard work is picking potatoes
and bagging them up in sacks,
then stacking them on the trailer,
it's enough to break your back.

Hard work is keeping on going
when everyone else is in bed.
You keep the midnight oil burning,
and check all the stock in the shed.

Hard work is when you've been mowing
grass for silage all day,
you know that a storm is brewing,
but all you can do is pray.

Hard work is being so tired that
you struggle to know who you are,
with back and tired muscles aching,
it's the toughest lifestyle by far.

Hard work is getting a call out
at night in the eye of a storm,
rounding up runaway heifers
and bringing them safely back home.

You may wonder why we do it,
face challenges others would hate,
get cut and bashed and filthy,
you may not think that it's great.

But when you see the moments
that make it all worthwhile,
the cows knee deep in fresh straw
with calves, you have to smile.

The silage rolled and covered
in a satisfying big clamp.
The first lambs of the season,
chicks warming under a lamp.

The grain store full to bursting,
Dutch barns stacked full of straw.
The glow of our achievements,
who could ever want for more.

It seems to be par for the course these days to have the most peculiar complaints about farming. Some are funny and some just unbelievable!

Complaints

Many grumble about noisy tractors,
rattling along country lanes.
We wish we could manage without them,
it would be fun if we could use planes.
Others moan that we have our cattle
crossing the road twice a day.
They have to go in for milking,
Can we please try another way?
Complaints include cows mooing,
in fields behind a new house.
We have done what we can to stop them;
told them to be quiet as a mouse.
Some others don't like the aromas,
which come when we stir the manure.
Cows seem to have always been smelly,
but we're searching hard for a cure.
Others tell us at night during harvest,
that we keep our tractors lights on.
We have tried to do it without them,
but Tom hit a bullock head on.
Then sometimes if it's been raining,
we're told that there's mud on the road,
and someone just phoned in to tell us
they're worried the sheep may be cold.

And would it be too much trouble
to make sure horses are brought in at night?
Mrs Buxton was sat on her decking,
and a mare made her jump up in fright.
Mrs Wallis was really quite tetchy,
when we needed to go through a gate.
because she was having a picnic,
and had just set out all her plates.
We were told at the village meeting,
that the Rowneys from number four
had witnessed us help a cow calving,
and were worried that she might be sore.
They said that we don't understand that
dogs like chasing sheep, it's good fun,
they love to run around playing,
so why did we bring out that gun?
So next time you visit some farmland,
remember we're trying our best,
to work and keep everyone happy,
so forgive us if we look stressed!

We all know some people like this. Some stick it out and learn the hard way and others give up and go back to the big city. We can't be too hard on them for wanting to live the good life, but it can be a lot harder than it first appears!

The good life

Have you met the family from Croydon
who have bought 30 acres of moor?
they now live in a chocolate box cottage
with roses around the door.
They have spent all their lives earning money
to buy up their country estate,
they've read all they know about farming,
they've had their names engraved on their gate.
They say that they want to keep chickens,
and have spent two thousand pounds on a coop,
it's got a designer pop hole so the birds don't have to stoop.
They've invested in Galloway cattle and kune kune pigs,
and have cleared apple trees from the orchard
so they can plant grapevines and figs.
They want to get fifty Jacobs, so that all their clothes can be wool,
but with only thirty acres their land is getting quite full.
They have bought a brand new Kubota to drive around the yard,
but the daughter filled it with petrol and is feeling rather scarred.
She thought that farming was easy she'd seen it on Countryfile,
but when she got stuck in the muck heap it really wasn't her style.
We saw them out there fencing, in designer jackets and hats
I overheard what my son called them, but I said enough of that!
When their pigs escaped through a thicket,we couldn't help but laugh,
especially when they told us, they took them home for a bath!
They have bought two springer spaniels to go with their rustic look,
we have seen them trying to train them, we giggled till we shook.

They ordered the cattle some jackets to stop them getting wet,
now they all have pneumonia and a great big bill from the vet.
We really shouldn't knock them for wanting to follow their dream,
but living out in the country isn't as easy as it first seems!

This is for all the parents who have endured the highs and lows of taking their children to a horse show.

The summer village horse show

It's the summer village horse show, the chance to get a rosette,
but for pony owning parents it brings on a nasty cold sweat.
Samantha from the Manor bought a pony for three thousand pounds,
it came with designer numnahs and a guarantee of a clear round.
Sophie from the Rectory has acquired a prize winning horse,
she likes to look down on others, but has yet to complete a course.
Jeremy has a new hunter and is finding it hard to ride,
it threw him off at the first fence, which really damaged his pride.
Daisy from the Old Dairy has a pony as slow as a cow,
she'd love to go a bit faster, but the pony doesn't know how.
Katie has a small piebald with a staring strange wall eye,
if it sees as much as a shadow, you know that it will shy.
David's horse gets excited as soon as it gets in the ring,
he tries his best to stay on it, but it's like riding a coiled spring.
Martha is riding Dark Shadow who's a sprightly thirty two,
but she's had to pull out of jumping because he's lost a shoe.
Kitty is having a panic because her pony doesn't have brakes,
she's flying round the cross country, she can't afford a mistake.
Rosie has taken to sulking because her pony refuses to move,
her best friend has won the dressage and she has a lot to prove.
Emma fell off at the water, it was such a terrible shame,
she hadn't tightened her girth up, so has had to accept the blame.
Jamie's horse had bolted and he disappeared fast up the hill,
his mother's developed a migraine and is feeling rather ill.
The prizes have been awarded, rosettes are proudly displayed,
loose ponies have been captured and all join in the parade.

The summer village horse show has been a great success,
but for pony owning parents it had its share of stress.
At least there is the option, if things haven't gone as planned,
to try the clear round jumping for a pink rosette in hand.
Then all will go home happy with dreams of the perfect horse,
though most would probably settle for getting round the course!

Farmers are a rare breed indeed. When they are away from the farm they are usually quite easy to spot! I think we all know someone who fits this description!

How to spot a farmer

Can you spot a farmer when they're far from home?
They're the ones sat in a corner talking silage on the phone.
The one whose golden sun tan stops half way up the arms,
the guy or girl with calloused hands, they're the one's who farm.

And if you are in London, they'll look you in the eye,
say "Morning folks, the sun is up, it looks like it'll be dry".
The ones who look frustrated whenever there's a queue,
if there are more than twenty folk. They don't know what to do.

They're be wearing their clean jacket that they've had since '83,
get fingers stuck in china cups whilst they're having tea.
And when they're out for dinner, it's eaten in a trice,
if it seems a bit expensive they will moan about the price.

And if you see them shopping, they'll be bright red in the face.
Sleeves rolled up, jumper off, they cannot take the pace.
They're used to striding forward not dodging prams and cars,
they do not like the noise and fuss, that's just the way they are.

So if you spot a fellow farmer whilst you are in the city,
nod and smile for they will know, they will share your pity.
They will be so thankful when they return to fields and barns
back from the crowded conurbations to the haven that's their
farm!

I grew up in the days before health and safety. Although we laugh at all the rules and regulations that tie us up in red paper, safety on farms has definitely improved over the years. The main problem facing farmers these days is the fact that they often have to work alone. Stay safe everyone!

Health and Safety

Cows that like kicking and bulls that are frisky,
farming has always been known to be risky.
Working alone in far distant places,
climbing high ladders with sweat on our faces.

Losing your footing when climbing up straw bales,
driving on gears when the old tractor's brakes fail.
Cutting up trees that have fallen on roads,
trailers piled high with unsecured loads.

Slurry lagoons with a thin crusty topping,
axes and wedges for logs that need chopping.
Sheep on the railway in the dead of the night,
splitting up dogs that have got in a fight.

Boars that are randy and sows that are evil,
make you jump higher than Evel Knievel.
Getting stuck in a bog which you just didn't see,
Ramblers that wave as you're having a pee.

Balancing crates on the old fore end loader,
mowing a field when you hit a big boulder.
Rolling the silage right up to the edge,
horses who bolt through a gap in the hedge.

Riding on loads and dodging low branches,
no one to help so you have to take chances.
Burning your hand when you weld up a gate,
sitting on bonnets to balance the weight.

Cutting your thumb when out trimming feet,
choking on dust when harvesting wheat.
Skinning your shin on an old rusty bucket
trying to say ouch when you want to say f**k it!

Farming's a risk, so make sure you've a grip,
on your boots and wellies and do up your zip.
Tie up your trousers and tuck loose ends away,
and you'll return in one piece at the end of the day!

I was asked if I could write a poem to be read out in our church for the harvest festival service. This is the one they got. On the next page is the alternative harvest poem, which you can probably relate to better than this one!

Harvest

Ploughing, harrowing, sowing, growing,
combine harvesting, sunsets glowing.
The culmination of all they planned,
reward for those who farm the land.

Golden grain fills up the trailers,
straw is packed up by the balers.
Church's fill with songs of praise,
to harvest home sweet voices raise.

Thanks to those who work the land,
who grow our food with their own hands.
Who work in sunshine, rain and snow,
who carry on when fierce winds blow.

Be grateful for your daily bread,
the eggs, the cheese, the jams we spread.
The milk, the butter from the dairies,
carrots, pears and fresh strawberries.

Pork and bacon, sausage rolls,
lamb and beef for casseroles.
fish, the harvest of the sea,
freshly caught for you and me.

We thank the ones who work the fields,
who work long hours to ensure yields.
the stockmen out there tending sheep.
The cowmen milking as we sleep.

The ones who farm far from our shores,
exotic fruits to fill our stores.
Tea and coffee in plantations,
the products of so many nations.

So now we say our thanks and praise,
to farmers working long hard days.
Let's raise a glass and celebrate,
the food we have upon our plate.

Whilst everyone is in church singing about harvest home, quite often the farmers are still out in the fields rushing to finish the job! Here is my alternative harvest poem.

Harvest home

Broken down combines, parts not in stock,
and the baler smashed a wheel when it hit a rock.
The cowman's sick, old Bert has been dragged out,
he is eighty four and suffers from the gout.

Ninety six more acres waiting to be cut,
the student's got his trailer turned over in a rut.
The church harvest festival is in full swing,
from underneath a bonnet I can hear the church bells ring.

They sing about the ploughs and the good seed on the land,
but we are still at work and could really use a hand.
There are calves to be fed and sheep to be moved,
they are singing our praises, but we are not amused.

Storm clouds gather, but there's work still to do,
the combine is patched together with string and glue.
It limps on slowly and bellows out black smoke,
gathering all in safely is becoming quite a joke.

Round and round the headland, up and down the track,
Old Bert's gone home with a twisted sore back.
The choir are singing about soft refreshing rain,
but the weatherman's forecast is a force 10 hurricane.

The harvest supper is held in the church hall,
the local village folk are having quite a ball.
but we don't mind if they've eaten all the grub,
because if we finish harvest, we're heading down the pub!

So many small dairy farmers have gone out of business recently. We need to be reminded sometimes that it is not just the cows we will miss if this continues.

The dairy farmer

Look out of your window,
Peer outside your door,
Green fields by the acre
Hedgerows by the score.

Cows there gently grazing,
Under age old trees.
Sunshine dappled shadows,
A gentle summers breeze.

Appreciate the beauty,
Admire the ancient views.
This way of life is threatened,
You've seen it in the news.

Farmed for generations,
So many have now left.
The prices paid to farmers,
Is tantamount to theft.

The massive supermarkets
Don't even pay their costs,
But many do not realise
And soon all will be lost.

Protect the dairy farmer,
Write to your MP,
Stand up and be counted
We need a guarantee.

Fair trade for British farming,
Should be our given right
So stand up for our farmers,
And help them win the fight!

So much has changed over the last fifty years or so. Here are a few memories from days gone by.

Country memories

Finger bar mowers, hedging and ditching,
scything and threshing and stooks that need pitching.
Lambing at night by a hurricane lamp,
carrots and parsnips in a dry sandy clamp.

Roguing the cornfields with a bag on your back,
loading potatoes in hessian sacks.
Hand hoeing turnips with the sun in your eyes,
harvesting mangolds under dark leaden skies.

Milking the shorthorns with a bucket and stool,
long before parlours and bulk tanks did rule.
Selling the milk fresh from the cow,
we wouldn't be able to do this all now.

Freshly dressed poultry with giblets for taste,
old boiler hens in the pot with no waste.
Salted green beans in used sweet shop jars,
ponies and traps in the days before cars.

Pickling, jamming, salting and drying,
seasonal harvests were so satisfying.
planning ahead for the long winter nights,
candles at bedtime, a soothing soft light.

Killing a pig and using each scrap,
Gran in the corner having a nap.
chitterlings and faggots, sweetbreads and tripe,
pigeons and partridge, occasional snipe.

Skinning a rabbit for a cheap hearty stew,
pearl barley with mutton from a worn out old ewe.
Black leaded grates that never went out,
poaching in rivers for salmon and trout.

Church on a Sunday in our Sunday best,
this was the day on which we could rest.
Back in the day our old shire pulled the plough,
I think he'd be shocked at what pulls them now.

Our last village meeting went on for over two hours, with many of the same issues being thrashed out over and over again. Many thought I was sat the back taking notes, but this poem is the result of my boredom!

The Annual village meeting

It's the annual village meeting
and Mr Drake is kicking off.
The tractors have been dusty
and they've given him a cough.

Mrs Ford is very vocal
she had found an empty can,
and she's written down the number
of a speeding parcel van.

There are issues about new houses,
from the Pritchards in the Grove.
They're worried they may glimpse them
whilst they're standing by their stove.

The local district council rep'
says we really must object.
If enough folk get together
the plans they might reject.

Mrs Truman is quite worried
that crime is on the rise,
she'd seen the milkman in a hoodie
and she'd screamed out with surprise.

The pothole by the churchyard
has been getting rather big,
the vicar saw a road-man,
but he didn't give a fig.

The meeting's in the village church
and the pews are very hard,
but they're moaning about manholes
protruding from a yard.

The local police inspector
tells us to lock our sheds.
We mustn't bring out shot guns
but use cameras instead.

We've elected a new chairman,
the same one as before.
When he asked us for a new one
we all looked at the floor.

And Pamela in the rectory
is fed up with the smell.
The farmer has been spreading muck
and she now feels quite unwell.

If we don't go to the meetings
we find we're volunteered,
to run the village party
and make sure the hall is cleared.

So we sit and numb our bottoms
and try to stay awake.
We ignore the same old rumblings
whilst we have our tea and cake!

Sheep farming certainly has its challenges as many of you will know only too well!

Sheep

It seems that a sheep's main ambition,
is to find different ways to drop dead.
You'd think their mates had just dared them,
before they're let out of the shed.

They'll throttle themselves in netting,
they'll drown on their backs in a mire,
they'll gorge on rotten old turnips,
and inflate like a blown up old tyre.

They'll succumb to all types of illness,
get fly strike that poisons their blood.
They'll ingest old nails whilst they're grazing,
then throw themselves into a flood.

And if you are not oh so careful,
they'll hang themselves in the yard,
even though you've cleared up the rubbish,
they will really try very hard.

And if they get out they will head for
the nearest main road or train track.
and every last one will follow,
not one will ever turn back.

It seems that if you're a shepherd,
you'll know every trick in the book.
But I wonder what their next plan is,
I think you'd best go take a look!

Old farmers experienced a different style of farming to the modern methods. The love of the land stays with us forever. This is the story of one old farmer, finally reunited with his beloved Betty.

Old Harry

He sits in his chair, his head bowed low,
remembering the years so long ago.
His body is now broken, his eyes don't see,
but in his mind his soul runs free.
The years of farming, following the plough,
he knew the names of each and every cow.
the precious summers when he was a boy,
each cherished memory gives him joy.
The hours spent hedging, ditching and mowing,
the sun on his face, the fresh wind blowing.
The sweet smell of hay he can still recall,
his old shire Sam, tethered in the stall.
A tear rolls down his tired old face,
he remembers each inch of his beloved space.
The meadows and hedges, the sparkling streams,
he closes his eyes and sees them in his dreams.
Now once again he is young and strong,
walking the hill sides, whistling a song.
with Tess his dog close by his side,
and his beautiful Betty who he made his bride.
He smiles and takes one last breath,
he is now not afraid of facing death.
His body remains, but he is set free,
the lock is broken he has found the key.

Another one now will farm his land,
they will know what to do, they will understand.
Remember him with a smile, don't be sad,
he was ready to go and for that we must be glad.

There are times in our lives when we need the support of someone special. I hope you all have someone who is there for you when the storms of life blow.

I will be there.

I will be your overcoat when the cold winds start to blow.
I will be your shelter when you have nowhere to go.
I will be your anchor when you're drifting far from shore,
I will be your friend when you can't take any more.

I will be your life boat when you are lost far out to sea,
I will unlock your shackles and try to set you free.
I will be a tiny candle to light your darkest night,
I will be your army when you can't face the fight.

I will be your light house to guide you when you're lost,
I will be a ray of sunshine to melt away the frost.
I will spark the glowing embers when your fire is burning low,
I will plant seeds of hope where you think they cannot grow.

If you are not a farmer you may admire the view, but not always realise the work involved in farming the land.

More than a view.

Muddy wellies in the porch,
leggings, twine, a high beam torch.
Straw on socks, cracked dry hands,
the marks of those who work the land.

Early mornings, late night rounds,
the stock you lost, the one's you found.
The harsh wind blowing through the night,
the fresh calved cows, a precious sight.

Days spent chasing missing sheep,
the promise of a good nights sleep.
Bales of hay to break your back,
safe in the barn, a tidy stack.

Rolling, harrowing, ploughing, sowing,
heavy rain that stops you mowing.
Diesel, oil and tubs of grease,
it seems the work will never cease.

The heartbreak of TB reactors,
the hours spent mending leaky tractors.
Relentless sun when you need rain,
Combines to harvest dusty grain.

The price of milk, the cost of feed,
the markets fed by others greed.
The joy of cows turned out in spring,
with gates secured by bits of string.

Sweet steaming silage in the feeder.
Ducks in a line play follow my leader.
The smells, the sights,the new born lambs,
far from the crowds and traffic jams.

To those who farm it's more than just
a job where you can earn a crust.
The land, the fields are in our blood,
it's more than slurry, muck and mud.

The hills and hedgerows, forests green,
are more than just a stunning scene.
They are our home, our work place too,
Farms are much more than just a view!

It is so frustrating to see supermarkets brimming with cheap imported food. We all need to support our local farmers wherever we live!

Buy British!

Danish bacon, New Zealand lamb,
no one seems to give a damn.
Dutch tomatoes, Polish pork,
check what's on your knife and fork.
German yoghurt, Brazilian beef.
Please turn over a new leaf.
Next time you go out to the shops,
look for British meat and crops.
Chicken from Thailand, apples from France,
They don't give us a fighting chance.
Shops packed full of foreign meat,
prices slashed, we can't compete.
You need to know what you are buying
read the labels, we are complying.
the highest standards on the earth,
are grown and bred on British turf.
Pick the packs with union flags,
red tractor labels; fill your bags.
Top quality is for you assured,
and our farm futures then secured.

And finally....

I could have been...

I could have been a sailor and sailed the seven seas,
I could have been a film star and gone just where I pleased.
I could have learned photography, with my pictures in the press,
or been a famous opera star in sparkling evening dress.

I could have been a doctor and cured a strange disease,
I could have learned psychiatry and put your mind at ease.
I could have been a soldier and learned to drive a tank,
I could have lived in London and worked inside a bank.

I could have been all kinds of things but I already knew,
that I would be a farmer, there was nothing else I'd do.
When you live upon the land it gets inside your head,
it's in your blood and in your soul, a farmer born and bred!

Lightning Source UK Ltd.
Milton Keynes UK
UKOW07f0614010516

273266UK00006B/26/P